50 Powerful Romantic Gestures That Will Make Your Partner Melt

By: Jordan Gray

www.JordanGrayConsulting.com

Copyright © 2015 Jordan Gray

Formatted by Archangel Ink

ISBN: 1515052966
ISBN-13: 978-1515052968

Table of Contents

Who This Book Is For 1

Note from the Author 2

How This Book Is Organized 4

The Importance of Implementation 5

Anatomy of a Romantic Gesture 6

The Intention behind a Powerful Romantic Gesture 10

Times That Call for Romantic Gestures 11

Gestures of Praise and Appreciation 13

Gestures of Service 23

Excursions and Adventures 35

Romantic Gifts 42

Quality Time and Connection 57

A Reminder to Take Action 63

Want to Become the Ultimate Relationship Partner? 64

One Last Thing 65

Other Books by Jordan Gray 66

About the Author 67

Who This Book Is For

This book is for any person who wants to bring more romance into their lives.

I have written this book from a gender-neutral perspective because I believe that any person—of any gender and any orientation—can benefit from having more romance in their lives, whether it's created by them or gifted to them by their partner.

Note from the Author

One of the most common questions I get asked in my coaching practice is, "How can I bring the spark back into our relationship?"

One of the answers to this query is that if you want more love in your relationship, you must be more loving. One way to be more loving is to introduce more loving, romantic gestures into your regular routine—which is not to say that the gestures themselves will come to feel like routines in the monotonous/predictable sense of the word. As you'll soon come to read in the pages of this book, surprise is almost always a necessary element in executing a powerful romantic gesture.

But if you're ever had the thought, "I want to do something nice for my partner/spouse/significant other" and not been sure of what to do, this book is for you.

In this book, you will find fifty powerful romantic gestures that have all been personally tested by me, hundreds of my readers, and a countless number of my private coaching clients. These gestures are all thoroughly tested so you can rest assured that they will be well received. That being said, your partner will respond to some of these gestures much more strongly than others, and that kind of calibration and awareness is where your responsibility in this process takes place. I have given you the ingredients and assembled them into gourmet meals, but it is up to you to know whether or not your unique romantic partner has specific food preferences that they have let you know about throughout the course of your relationship.

If you've ever been stuck for something romantic to do (whether for a birthday, anniversary, Valentine's Day, or just a regular old Tuesday afternoon) when you wanted it the most, this book has you covered. Highlight your favorite romantic gestures with bookmarks or sticky notes, or simply open the book up to a random page whenever you're feeling the urge to bring more intentionality into your love life.

How This Book Is Organized

I have organized all of the romantic gestures to fit within five unique categories: gestures of praise and appreciation, gestures of service, romantic gifts, quality time and connection, and excursions and adventures.

Through each of the five sections, the romantic gestures have been ordered from the least challenging to implement to the most challenging to implement. None of the gestures have been made intentionally difficult to execute, but certain gestures definitely take more time, energy, or resources to create than others. So if you find yourself wanting to go for some quick, inexpensive, easy to implement gestures, scan the first half of each of the sections. On the other hand, if you want to go for the huge "WOW" factor, you might want to primarily look at the last few romantic gestures per section.

There is a huge range throughout this book, and while some romantic gestures will take less than five minutes to do (from reading it to presenting it to your partner), there are a couple of gestures that will take several months (or even years) to carry out to the fullest extent possible. You've been warned!

The Importance of Implementation

The words you're about to read are only powerful if you take action on them.

If you read all fifty gestures and yet you don't implement a single one of them, then your intimate relationship will not improve.

So please, for the love of love, read through the fifty gestures, pick your top two or three favorites, and then put them in your calendar as soon as possible in order to take action on them.

Implementing a single romantic gesture won't necessarily make or break your relationship, but over time, the effects of doing twenty versus doing zero will absolutely have a massive impact. So while it's important that you start small, it's even more important that you start at all.

Anatomy of a Romantic Gesture

All romantic gestures are not created equal. Here are five elements that you can aim to put into any romantic gestures you utilize in your relationship. The fifty gestures in this book already contain these elements, but just in case you want to create your own romantic gestures, the awareness of these five elements (and why each of these is uniquely important for creating the love that you desire) will help you get started.

Surprise

The element of surprise will be essential in the vast majority of romantic gestures that you use.

Predictability is a very comforting and beautiful part of being in any romantic relationship, but as humans, we all crave some predictability and routine AND some newness, novelty, and surprise.

More often than not, making your romantic gesture a surprise will bring the power of it up a notch. There are some gestures wherein you might have to give your partner some warning (a fancy night out for which they have to dress a certain way, a weekend excursion for which they will need to pack a bag, etc.), but for the most part, having them be a total surprise is the way to go.

Thought

It really is the thought that counts.

If your gesture (the one that you use from the pages of this book or the ones you create on your own) takes time, energy, and thoughtfulness, then you're likely on to something good.

Calibration

In order to be as powerful as possible, your romantic gesture needs to be calibrated to *your* partner.

If the romantic gesture that you use for your partner seems drastically disconnected from them, there is a high probability that it will fall flat.

They detest being outside for any length of time and you planned a weekend excursion of hiking and camping? No good.

They can only take a certain amount of physical contact until they start to feel overstimulated, and yet you planned a four-hour massage/pedicure/spa date for them? That might cause them more stress than bliss.

They prefer smaller, quieter events with a few close friends and you decided to plan them a 40-person surprise birthday party? You might be in trouble for a while if you go through with that one.

Take the time to think about what makes your partner feel uniquely appreciated. Some of the following fifty gestures will be exactly what your partner needs to feel loved, while other gestures won't be as relevant. That's fine. Use whatever is most useful for your specific partner. Or, as Bruce Lee once said, *"Adapt what is useful, reject what is useless, and add what is uniquely your own."*

Self-initiated

While romantic gestures can certainly have a positive effect on Valentine's Day or your partner's birthday, if your romantic gesture is self-initiated (meaning it happened because you decided to make it happen and not because the calendar told you that you should be romantic), then it is going to be that much more powerful.

Nine times out of ten, deploying a romantic gesture in order to love your significant other "just because I love you" will be better received than if the intention behind it is, "Well, it's Valentine's Day, and it's expected of me."

Taking the initiative in your love life will always be appreciated. Besides, your partner is worth it!

Simplicity

It's easy to get overwhelmed by the details of having to plan out a five-part date with chauffeurs, dinner reservations, long-stem roses, and candle-lit, champagne-fuelled sunsets… so keep it simple!

Shave off as many layers of complexity as possible for your romantic gesture to mean the most.

You don't need to spend a lot of money (or necessarily time) for your romantic gesture to speak volumes about how you feel about your partner.

As long as they feel any combination of loved, cared for, special, happy, or blissful, the romantic gesture will be a success.

The Intention behind a Powerful Romantic Gesture

Sometimes people assume that being romantic is some kind of trade-off. As if romance is a tool to be used for bartering.

If your romantic gesture has the underlying feeling of "I'll do this for them so that they will in turn have more sex with me/do the dishes more often/do something for me/etc.," then you're going about it all wrong.

The most powerful romantic gestures come exclusively from a place of love.

You implement a romantic gesture because you want your partner to feel good. You want to make their day. You want them to smile, cry tears of joy, or simply feel loved. If your intention is anything but one of the aforementioned things, it may very likely fall flat.

So give your love unconditionally.

Let your romantic gesture stand on its own two feet. Let it declare, "I did this simply because I love you, and I want you to feel amazing," and it is sure to be a success.

Times That Call for Romantic Gestures

While I have mentioned that I believe that any old day has the potential (and the right) to be a day worthy of a romantic gesture, here is a list of days / events / milestones that more specifically could be celebrated by you or your partner.

- Anniversary of when your relationship officially started
- Anniversary of your first date
- Anniversary of your first kiss
- Anniversary of the first time you were intimate together
- Wedding anniversary
- Celebrating a milestone in your career
- Celebrating a milestone in your partner's career
- Having kids
- Mother's Day or Father's Day
- Your birthday
- Your partner's birthday

- Valentine's Day/Christmas/major holidays that you or your partner celebrate
- The anniversary or beginning of major life transitions (career change, moving houses, changing cities/countries/locations, etc.)
- Monday
- Tuesday
- Wednesday
- Thursday

You get the point! Any day will do. Any day that you love your partner is a beautiful day to celebrate them and your relationship together.

So, you know what comprises a powerful romantic gesture, you know when you can use them… now, on to the romantic gestures themselves.

Like I mentioned earlier, these specific gestures have all been thoroughly relationship-tested, and I can personally attest to their greatness.

Not only have these served me well over the years, I've had over 30 of them make my partner cry tears of joy when I surprised her with these gestures.

There isn't a dud in the bunch. It's simply up to you to decide which ones will be the best received by your intimate partner.

Without further ado, here are the fifty powerful romantic gestures.

Enjoy!

Gestures of Praise and Appreciation

Does your partner respond the most strongly to the things you say to them or when you let them know how much you love them? Then this section is for you.

1. Miniature Love Note Surprise

Sporadically leave folded up single compliments in different places that you know they will come into contact with like their journal, purse, make-up kit, toolbox, kitchen drawers, lunch box, etc.

Watch Out For:

Similar to an Easter egg hunt, you want to leave your love notes in places that are obvious enough that they will find them within a week or two. That being said, if you leave so many around the house that you forget where they have all been placed, it wouldn't be the worst thing if they found an extra love note in an especially obscure location weeks, or even months, after you first placed the love notes around their life.

How to Multiply the Magic:

Keep the content of the love notes quite simple. One or two sentences will do. Compliment things that they are used to receiving compliments on and also on things that get praised far less often. Compliment their personality, their mind, their appearance, who they are as a person, and what they bring to your life. The options are truly endless.

2. Write Them an Epic Love Letter

If there's one romantic gesture that most consistently makes my partner cry tears of happiness, it's this one.

Invest some time in writing a long-form love letter (anywhere from 500-1,500 words should do the trick) and deliver it to them personally. You can either deliver it to them by hand and watch them read it, or you can read it out loud to them if you think that they would prefer to receive it that way.

Does writing not come naturally to you? Want a quick example of a structure that works well for writing a love note? Your wish is my command!

Start with why.

Personally, I love starting my love letters with a quick explanation of why I'm sending it. This can be as short as a few words or as lengthy as a few paragraphs.

For example, you could say any of the following to kick off your love letter:

> *"This letter is long overdue, and it's been tumbling around in my mind for weeks now. So I thought it was finally time to put pen to paper and tell you how I feel about you."*
>
> *"You do so many little things day to day that elevate my opinion of you. You are such a gift in my life, and you deserve to know it... so I decided to write you this letter."*
>
> *"I'm not so good with talking about my feelings sometimes, but I didn't want my thoughts to go unsaid... so I thought a letter would be best."*

Grounding the love letter with a reason can lead people into the experience of "get ready for this huge incoming smorgasbord of emotions!" by pacing their reality of "what am I about to read here?"

What do they bring to your life?

For this point, and the following five points, brainstorm your responses for as long as you need to. Give it its own few sheets of paper if you need to.

What exactly does your partner bring to your life? Think physically, emotionally, mentally, spiritually, and sexually. How do they elevate your life? How do they make your daily existence that much easier or better?

Maybe you've told them about certain ways, or maybe you've told them almost none of them. This is your chance. Brainstorm anywhere from 10-50 things that your partner brings to your life and then pick your favorite handful to focus on.

Some examples could be:

> *"I love how you encourage the best parts of me. I am healthier, more driven, and more emotionally fulfilled than at any other point in my life, and that is in large part because of you."*
>
> *"Thank you so much for reminding me who I am when I sometimes forget. I am so grateful to have you as a rock in my life."*
>
> *"You have helped me turn my dreams into a reality in so many areas of my life. You are an absolute blessing."*

As always, make sure that it's true for YOU. Calibration is key. And, by all means, if any of the above examples do ring true for you, then please feel free to use them verbatim.

Allude to memories that you share.

Do you have a pre-existing relationship with this person? Write out a list of your favorite memories with them and pick the top couple of memories to reference in your love letter.

Examples:

> *"That one time that you laughed so hard that chocolate milk came out of your nose? I fell in love with you right then and there."*
>
> *"I can't believe it's already been two years since we went on that trip to (location) together. I have such fond memories of how we navigated the streets like a team, and we went the entire trip without even a small argument. We've always worked so well together as a couple, and I couldn't feel happier that we're together."*
>
> *"Our first kiss was so blissful that I thought I might fall over. My legs felt like jelly for the next few days. You certainly have always had a powerful effect on me."*

You can either allude to your multiple memories in a rapid-fire, one- to two-sentence format, or you can really sit with one amazing memory and describe it in vivid detail. The choice is yours.

What do you love about them?

A slight variation on point #2, what specifically do you love about the person you're writing to?

What do you love about their character, their appearance, or what they fill their life with? Brainstorm/jot it down, and then let them know what you consider to be the highlights.

Examples of what you might love about them:

> *"I love your drive and ambition. I have endless faith that you'll achieve anything you put your mind to."*
>
> *"You are so amazingly loyal to those you care about. The depth with which you love others is nothing short of inspiring. I love your massive heart."*
>
> *"I don't think I actually had a sex drive before I met you. You are the sexiest thing in the world, and I couldn't be more attracted to everything about you."*
>
> *"You are so thoughtful with me. I noticed that you did (X), (Y), and (Z), recently, and I want you to know that I notice all of it."*
>
> *"Your eyes are so captivating. I could get lost in them forever." "You are simply the best person I have ever known. I have endless respect for you and the way that you carry yourself in this world. So thank you for being you."*

What do they not get told enough by you (or by anyone)?

I call this the Elusive Obvious effect. Often, the things that are presented most obviously are the things that get taken for granted the most.

Also, if you are more prone to complimenting them on just one thing or one area (i.e., only their physical appearance, or only one of the things that they bring to your life), then this can be a good exercise for expanding your awareness of all of the other things that you love about them.

The devil's in the details.

While it's nice to praise the things hidden in plain view, I find that the most memorable moments in love letters come from finding the super specific details that you love about the love letter recipient and letting them be known. Just imagine… your love letter could be the first time anyone has let them know that they have some specific gift that they bring to another's life. And every time they notice that detail about themselves, the thought will be linked back to you and your thoughtful letter.

Really sit and brainstorm with this one. What are the teensy, tiny, detailed things that your love letter recipient does/is that make your heart light up? It could be the way that they laugh, the way they eat, or the way they tear up when you're watching a certain movie together. I wish I could give you a laundry list of 200 things for you to pull from, but you know your love letter recipient infinitely better than I do. Really give this specific exercise some time. The few nuggets of gold that you mine from your brain will pay dividends in your relationship for years to come if you do this one right.

Plans for the future.

I like to finish my love letters with this element, but you can put them throughout your letter as you see fit.

Let them know that you're in the relationship for the long haul by alluding to some imagined future plans that you want to see come to fruition.

Maybe it's the fact that you'll have children one day… or a trip to Paris that you want to take in a few years… or kissing each other's wrinkly old faces. Whatever it is, make it something that you're authentically excited about for your shared future.

Watch Out For:

Even though you're looking to write a long-form love letter, you want to make sure that you don't drone on for too long. I find that somewhere around the 1,000-word mark is sufficient.

By all means, write a letter that is as long as you need to convey the message that you need to... but if you're starting to venture into your fourth, fifth, or sixth page of words, you might want to consider reigning it in a bit and going for quality over quantity. More is not necessarily better when it comes to love notes.

How to Multiply the Magic:

The biggest thing I would recommend doing for this gesture versus many of the others in this book would be to really take your time in the creation of it. If words of praise and appreciation mean a lot to your partner, this could be a gift that they repeatedly come back to and read throughout your entire relationship. So spend some time writing it, get it professionally edited if you feel so inclined, and read it out loud to a few of your close friends and family members before you give it to your significant other to get their opinions (just make sure that you tell those test-listeners to keep your love letter writing a secret).

3. The "100 Things I Love About You" List

If you're more of a bullet-point type of writer, or your partner is more logical and structured than most people, then this format of delivering praise and appreciation might work better for them.

Write up a list of 100 things that you love about your partner and frame it in a beautiful frame.

You can even subcategorize the things that you love about them into ten different sections. You can include section headlines/themes such as "How You Are with Your Friends," "How You Are in Your Work Life," and "How You Are with Me," and then provide ten examples of things that you love about them under each of those section headlines. As always, calibrate your theme and compliments to your significant other as best as you can.

Watch Out For:

Repetitiveness. While there may be some natural overlap in the things that you're complimenting your partner on, make sure that you're not simply rewording the same ten things over and over. Dig deep to find some variety in what it is that you love about them.

How to Multiply the Magic:

Have the layout of the piece of paper professionally designed to have a photo of you and your partner as the faint background behind the words.

4. Love Note Mason Jar

Write 365 love notes and put them in a beautifully decorated mason jar. This way, your partner can either open one love note per day for the entire year, or they can binge in one sitting by reading about all of the beautiful things that you have said about them.

How to Multiply the Magic:

Use different colored pieces of paper for your love notes (use a minimum of five different colors… light pastel colors tend to work well), tie a silk ribbon around the top of the jar, and/or put sparkles on top of the lid.

5. Newspaper Surprise

Take out an ad in the paper telling the world why you love your partner so much. Even if your partner doesn't read the newspaper that day, if the newspaper has enough of a reach in your city, one (or several) of their friends will be sure to point it out to them.

Watch Out For:

Typos! Check, double-check, and triple-check your piece before you send it in to the newspaper.

How to Multiply the Magic:

Take out a full-page ad in the paper for increased "Wow" factor.

Gestures of Service

Does your partner most frequently light up from the sweet things that you *do* as opposed to the things that you say or give them? Then this section is for you!

6. Layered Love

Prove to them that chivalry isn't dead.

If it's cold outside and you know that your partner is underdressing for the weather, make sure that you wear an extra layer so that it's easy for you to give them your coat when they inevitably get cold. This one never goes out of style. It's chivalrous, protective, and loving.

7. The Warm Towel Wrap-Up

While your significant other is in the shower, put their towel in the dryer so that they have a nice hot towel for when they get out. This is a simple gesture that goes a long way. It shows them that you think of them and their comfort.

Watch Out For:

Two things to watch out for:
1. Make sure that you deliver the towel on time. As soon as you hear them switch off the water, grab the towel and race it over to them so that it's nice and toasty.
2. If you sneakily grab the towel out of the bathroom while they're in the shower (to throw it in the dryer), make sure that you don't forget about the gesture midway through and leave them stepping out of the shower to no towel.

How to Multiply the Magic:

Present them with the warm towel and bring them their favorite hot drink at the same time (tea, coffee, hot chocolate, etc.).

8. Foot Rub Romance

Surprise them one night by dimming the lights, putting on one of their favorite relaxing albums, and giving them an extended foot rub.

Watch Out For:

Rubbing their feet with too much strength or too little strength. Check in with them near the beginning (in the first minute or two) to see if the pressure is good for them.

How to Multiply the Magic:

Give them two or three different scented options of oils or lotions. Pick a variety so that you can use whatever they're most in the mood for. A good place to start would be selecting any of your favorites from the following: lavender, chamomile, vanilla, cinnamon, peppermint, citrus, jasmine, and good old-fashioned unscented oil.

9. Surprise Stock of Snacks and Sippers

Stock up your fridge and pantry with all of their favorite drinks and snacks. Do this gesture while they're out of the house running errands. When they return, don't call any attention to the fact that you've done it. Just let them find it for themselves. The surprise is sure to delight them!

Watch Out For:

Don't do this in the middle of them being on a strict diet or you might just be unfairly tempting them.

How to Multiply the Magic:

Go out of your way to find specific items (that you know they love) that are not readily accessible in your city. The more effort you put into this gesture, the better. And a wide variety of snack and drinks options that they love is always great. Aim for five units of five different snack options, and ten units of their five favorite drinks.

10. The Warm Awakening

This gesture works even better if you're a morning person and your partner isn't.

Go to a nearby coffee shop and bring them back their favorite drink to wake up to in bed (coffee, mocha, hot chocolate, latte, etc.).

Watch Out For:

Make sure you know exactly what their favorite drink is to begin with! Whether it's a hot beverage like coffee, tea, mocha, hot chocolate, or a latte, or a cold beverage like a particular smoothie, cold-pressed juice, or coconut water, get absolute clarity about what their favorite drink is and then go and grab it for them. The devil's in the details. And while it would still be a romantic gesture if you brought them the *almost* correct drink, they'll feel that much more seen and loved if you nail it with 100% accuracy (especially if they're picky about their drink).

Also, make sure you get the drink for them around the time when they would naturally start to wake up. If you show up with their favorite caffeinated drink at a time that is three hours before they would normally want to start their day, they might not be as pleased with you.

How to Multiply the Magic:

Gently kiss them awake, and then surprise them with the drink (either in your hand or on the bedside table). To call attention to the drink (should you decide to put it on the bedside table), a simple and playful, "Oh, who put that there?" will suffice.

11. Drink Drop-Off

If they're going to be seated in one place for a while outside of the house (like getting their nails done or getting their hair cut) drop in, as a surprise, and bring them their favorite drink with a straw.

Watch Out For:

Delivering a hot drink that's so hot that they might burn their tongue when they take their first sip.

12. Lunch Box Lovin'

Pack your partner an elaborate lunch one day for work. For example, you could pack their favorite meal, a cold drink, and a few squares of dark chocolate. Now who wouldn't love to indulge in that during their lunch break?

Watch Out For:

Food allergies or including any items that they don't enjoy.

How to Multiply the Magic:

Include a short love note and a photo of the two of you kissing.

13. Breakfast in Bed

Wake them up with a surprise breakfast in bed! And if their diet allows, make heart-shaped pancakes and bacon. Take heart-shaped cookie cutters, place them on the griddle, and pour your pancake batter into them. Once they've cooked enough on that side, they should be firm enough for you to be able to flip them over. Voila! Perfectly heart-shaped pancakes!

Watch Out For:

Make sure that you deliver the food around a time they would naturally want to wake up. You don't want them to be so groggy that they barely remember the gesture.

How to Multiply the Magic:

Include their favorite drink, a love note, and a small bouquet of flowers along with breakfast delivery.

14. Become a Chef for a Day

Make them their favorite meal from scratch. Is their favorite meal something that is inherently more difficult to create (like fish and chips, crème brûlée, or a specific type of burger with a hard to find protein)? Perfect! You'll get extra brownie points for attempting it. It doesn't have to be the best they've ever had; just the thought of you trying to recreate it is a romantic gesture. That being said, do your best to make it as delicious as possible.

Watch Out For:

Ruining the meal. If you're feeling really intimidated, ask some of your more culinarily inclined friends for advice.

How to Multiply the Magic:

Wear a chef apron or set of professional whites while you're making it to add to the chef effect.

15. Do ALL of the Chores

For those who are especially taken by gestures of service, there isn't much better you can do than this one.

On a day when you know they'll be out of the house for at least four to six hours, do every chore that you can think of around your house/their house.

Do all of the laundry, clean every surface, vacuum, tidy up, take out the garbage and the recycling, replace burned out light bulbs, and fix anything that needs to be fixed or updated.

Just imagine the look of shock, surprise, and delight when your partner comes home to see everything spotless, completed, and shiny!

Watch Out For:

When you're tidying up, make sure that you don't throw anything away that they might actually want to keep.

How to Multiply the Magic:

Combine this gesture with the pantry-filling gesture mentioned earlier in the book. Do all of the chores AND fill the fridge and pantry with all of their favorite snacks and drinks. For someone who loves gestures of service, they will likely cry tears of joy at how sweet and thoughtful of a partner you are.

16. Make Your Bedroom a Sleeping Sanctuary

Did you know that certain color temperatures of light can interfere with your sleeping patterns?

To make sure that you and your significant other get the best rest possible, change all of the light bulbs in your bedroom to a warm color temperature. The color temperature of bulbs that you'll be looking for when you go to your local lighting and/or hardware store is "tungsten" (and you'll want to avoid/remove any "daylight" color temperature bulbs from your room).

As a bonus, you can also install blackout blinds over any of your bedroom windows to keep the natural light out.

Watch Out For:

Run these changes by your partner first since they might want to know that you're doing it before you implement these changes to your room.

How to Multiply the Magic:

Invest in incense or aromatherapy scented oils to give the room a nice relaxing scent (lavender, jasmine, and chamomile are often good scents to relax your mind and body).

17. Add Value to Their Extended Social Network

This is something that I love talking about since it is so powerful and yet it almost never gets mentioned anywhere.

The people that your significant other holds close to their heart matter a lot to them. So do something kind and loving for someone they hold dear. It might even mean just as much (if not more) to them as if you had done any of these gestures for them.

Some examples?

Help a family member of theirs with something that has been an obstacle of theirs for a while, buy a small gift for their pet, babysit your partner's nieces or nephews in order to give their siblings an evening off from their parenting duties, etc.

Long story short, add value to the lives of those your loved one holds close to their heart. It might just affect them more than you could have ever imagined.

18. Relax and Unwind

In advance of your partner returning home from work (or just a long day of errands), draw them a bath and set the scene for a nice, relaxing sanctuary for them to unwind in.

Watch Out For:

Make sure you get the water temperature right. By this point in your relationship, you likely know what level of heat they like in their water (you *have* showered together, haven't you?), so do your best to mimic that water temperature in the water.

How to Multiply the Magic:

Add a few drops of their favorite essential oil to the water. Sprinkle a few dozen rose petals over the surface of the water. Place some lightly scented candles around the room (to avoid having an unattended fire hazard, only light them after they've entered the room). Offer to hand-feed them pieces of their favorite snack while they have their long, luxurious soak.

If you want to really kick it up a notch, you can even ask if they would like you to either wash their hair for them, give them a foot massage, or both!

19. Spa Night In!

Spas are great, but not everyone has hundreds of dollars to drop on an all-day spa package. Plus, this romantic gesture packs a personal punch.

Plan a spa night where you give your partner a foot massage, pedicure, gentle exfoliating scrub, facial, and back massage.

Watch Out For:

Be mindful about the fact that there might be some spa procedures that your partner doesn't particularly enjoy. Do they not like having their feet touched because they're too ticklish? Then the pedicure might be out of the question. Do they have sensitive skin and an exfoliating scrub might be more stressful than relaxing for them? Then skip that step! As always, the more calibrated it is to your partner and their specific needs, the better.

Whatever things you include in your spa day, make sure that you have all of the tools, creams, and lotions that you might need beforehand. And always have multiple options for anything scented (moisturizers, massage oils, etc.) just in case they don't like one of the scents that you're about to use.

If you're ever in doubt about a particular scented product, check with your partner first before you use it. After all, this gesture is all about them and their comfort.

How to Multiply the Magic:

Make sure to have several hours of relaxing music on hand. Also, kombucha, red wine, green tea, and lemon water are always good to have on hand.

Excursions and Adventures

Does your partner feel the most loved and cared for when you plan things for the two of you to do together? Then this section is for you!

20. Slow Dance at Sunset

Get your hands on a portable music player (playable not just through headphones but through audible speakers), equip it with you and your partner's song or an album that you both fell in love to, drive out to somewhere beautiful, and slow dance to your music.

How to Multiply the Magic:

Kick it up a notch by driving out and doing this at sunset. Or, if you're both early morning people and/or really active, hike somewhere beautiful and scenic to catch the sun rising. If you decide to go with the morning hike, make sure that you keep the music player a secret by hiding it inside of a sweater in your backpack.

21. Passionate Picnic

Plan a picnic for the two of you with their favorite foods and write a short love note on their napkin.

Watch Out For:

Sunburns and bug bites! It's not sexy, but it'll be thoughtful of you to come prepared by packing sunscreen, sunglasses, and bug spray (especially if your area is prone to mosquitoes during good weather).

How to Multiply the Magic:

Pack a backpack/basket filled with the following:

- Two or three of their favorite snacks or sides
- Two sandwiches or whatever their favorite meal is
- Two plastic champagne glasses
- A miniature bottle of sparkling wine, cider, or champagne
- Two small portions of their favorite dessert
- Three napkins—one for you, one for them, and the bonus napkin for your partner with your personalized love note written on it
- A portable music player (and batteries) to play music that is either relevant to the two of you or super cheesy and romantic. If you go with the latter option, the more over the top it is, the better!

22. Rooftop Rendezvous

Does your city either have an airport, annual fireworks, or a beautiful nighttime view of the stars? With any of these three situations (or all three if you're an overachiever), you can pack a bag filled with blankets, hand warmers, hot chocolate or a half bottle of champagne, and drive out to a beautiful area and camp out on the hood of your car while you either watch planes landing, fireworks bursting into fragmented light, or twinkling stars.

Watch Out For:

The weather!

If your city gets cold at night, make sure you pack multiple blankets and hand warmers. Extra sweaters would be a safe bet as well.

23. Revisit Where Your Relationship Started

Celebrate your anniversary (6 month, 1 year, 3 year, 5 year, or any denomination of time that feels relevant) at the place where you first met or had your first date. Whether it's a restaurant or an outdoors location, it will still carry with it the magic of the first time you met.

Watch Out For:

If it's a restaurant or indoor venue, make sure you book a reservation well in advance and let them know what the occasion is.

How to Multiply the Magic:

If there's a specific table/spot/area where you first had your date, make sure that you specifically book it. You can even set it up in advance to have flowers, a love note, or a special gift waiting for them at their seat.

24. The Infamous Three Envelope Date Structure

If you've read my *50 Powerful Date Ideas* book, you might recognize this one. I've had so many of my friends, family, and clients use this date structure (and have amazing results) that I just had to include it in this book as well.

Here's the gist of it...

Write three different sets of date night plans on three different pieces of paper and enclose them in three separate envelopes. Once you've done this, have your significant other open only one of the envelopes... like a choose-your-own-adventure!

And even if they beg you to be able to look inside all three of the envelopes, don't let them! That would ruin the fun of it. This way, with the help of their choosing hand, the way your date night plays out was fated to be.

Watch Out For:

You have to make sure that whatever the three potential dates are, they are all possible. For example, if you include a certain restaurant as one of the options for the date night, call ahead to make sure that they have availability. If you plan to visit a bowling alley, make sure that they're not already fully booked up with pre-existing reservations.

There's nothing worse than getting your partner excited to go one of the dates that you've planned out and then finding out that the one that they chose was a dead-end (through no fault of their own).

How to Multiply the Magic:

Make each of the three potential date night plans multi-phase dates. So instead of just writing "movie," "dinner at this place," and "stay in and cuddle" on each of the three pieces of paper, one of the envelopes/sample date nights would say, "We start off with a walk down near this beach, grab an appetizer and glass of wine at this tapas bar, have dinner overlooking the water at this restaurant, and finish off the night by watching this romantic movie at our favorite movie theater."

25. "We're going to See Your Favorite…"

Buy them tickets to their favorite artist/musician/band. Gift the tickets to them as a surprise a few days in advance.

Watch Out For:

Make sure that they have the night off. Check in with your friends, their employer, and your shared calendar. Do whatever it takes to make sure that they are free that night. You can even subtly make sure they'll be available by telling them five to seven days in advance that you want to have a date night, and then surprising them with the specifics of the date a day or two beforehand.

How to Multiply the Magic:

If you have the connections or resources, see if you can arrange for a meeting between them and the artist(s). Whether you win it through a radio contest or score the connection through friends, if you never try, you'll never know. Many musicians are much more accessible than you'd think if you know where to look.

26. Photo Booth Fun

Plan a date night where you both have to dress up really nicely (like going to the opera or a nice restaurant) and make sure that you pass by a photo booth on your way. Pretending like you didn't know it was there, pull them into the photo booth and do two rounds of photos to keep as beautiful souvenirs of your amazing night out.

Watch Out For:

Make sure you are both in a good mood on the way to your date. Don't rush your partner in getting ready, because the camera will capture whatever mood you're both in.

How to Multiply the Magic:

Frame the two photograph strips in a beautiful frame and place it somewhere you can both see it in order to remember your beautiful date night.

27. A Weekend Getaway for Lovers

Secretly make plans for the two of you by booking a weekend excursion to a place that's within a few hours' drive of you (think spa, cabin, hiking… all of which are great for romantic connection). Make the sole intention for your weekend to deeply reconnect as a couple.

Watch Out For:

Distractions! The intention behind your weekend is to reconnect, so make sure you keep any and all life stuff away from you. No phones, no kids, don't bring work along with you… the weekend is just for the two of you.

Romantic Gifts

Does your partner respond the most strongly to the things that you physically give them? Then this section is for you!

28. The Inherent Magic of the Mixed Tape

Make them a mixed tape/cd/playlist of songs that has unique ties to your relationship or that remind you of them.

Watch Out For:

If you're someone who doesn't naturally listen to lyrics, make sure that you pay attention to the lyrics for this exercise. Look them up if you have to. There's nothing worse than accidentally including a song that is clearly about a break-up because you neglected to look into the lyrics/meaning behind the song. You don't want to send mixed messages!

How to Multiply the Magic:

If you gift them a physical hard copy of the gift (a tape, CD, etc.), you can design (or get someone else to design) a unique cover image to wrap the gift in. Whether it's a photo of the two of you, a photo collage of memories that you have together, or a cheesy looking photo of you holding a guitar, anything that will make your significant other smile will work perfectly.

29. Framed Photo Collage

Create a photo collage of the two of you and frame it. Not much of a graphic designer? You can always pay a friend or hire a Photoshop wizard to do it for you.

Watch Out For:

Don't include photos that you think they might not like themselves in. We all have a tendency to just look at ourselves in photos. Look at it from your partner's perspective and make sure that you think they would agree with every photo choice that you included.

30. Special Delivery for the Best Person in the World

Have flowers delivered to their place of work (or give them flowers just because).

Watch Out For:

Make sure you give them a bouquet of flowers that they love. Do they have a favorite flower? Then give them two-dozen of those. Do they like a certain color palate? Then give them a large assortment of those. If your relationship is newer and you're unsure of what to go with, choose between either a dozen red roses (classic romance) or a large assortment of pink, orange, yellow, and purple flowers. You can't go wrong with a big bouquet of colorful flowers!

How to Multiply the Magic:

If your partner doesn't embarrass easily (or they love lots of attention), you can have the person deliver the flowers via a singing telegram. It's a real thing! The delivery person will sing a personalized song for your beloved.

31. Airport Surprise!

If your partner is going to be coming back from a trip via a flight, tell them that you won't be able to greet them at the airport because of an unfortunate and unmovable scheduling issue (knowing full well that you'll be there to surprise them).

Then, show up at the airport with a bouquet of flowers, a gift, a hand-drawn banner, or any other surprise. If you want the surprise to speak for itself, your mere presence can be the gift. In which case, shower them with hugs and kisses.

Watch Out For:

Even though you tell them you won't be able to make it, make sure that none of their other friends or family have been called in to pick them up. It doesn't necessarily hurt to have more people there that love them to greet them at the airport, but you don't want to be wasting their friends' time unnecessarily when you know full well that you'll be there to greet them.

How to Multiply the Magic:

If you feel like organizing a welcoming committee, you can even have a dozen or so friends and family accompany you for the surprise. You don't have to wait for them to go on a long (or even distant) trip. It could be a domestic trip, and they will still welcome the surprise of being welcomed home by a group of their favorite people.

32. Wish upon a Star

Buy your partner a star and name it after them. Sound too good to be true? Your significant other will think so too!

This gesture is surprisingly easy to do. Search in your local area for things like "name a star," "buy a star," or "international star registry," and you'll be surprised at how easy (and inexpensive) it is to buy a star for someone.

Watch Out For:

The price often depends on how bright the star is and how frequently you are able to see it. So, if you know that your relationship has long-term potential, it might be worth it to spend over $100 (as opposed to some of the cheaper stars that can be acquired for under $20).

How to Multiply the Magic:

Name the star after your significant other (either their first name or a consistent pet name that you have for them).

33. The Month-Long Loving Lead-Up

Does your loved one have a birthday coming up? Or perhaps your anniversary is on the horizon?

When a significant occasion is six to eight weeks away, you better start planning! Send them a card every day for a month leading up to a major occasion and you'll blow them away.

Watch Out For:

Make sure that you're prepared going into this romantic gesture. Not everyone can write a letter a day off the top of their head, so it's good to pre-write at least half of your cards for them. That way you can reference things that happen naturally throughout the actual month, while also having a healthy volume of backup cards that will always be ready to gift them with. Also, make sure that you hand deliver the cards as opposed to sending them via any other delivery service because you are likely more reliable (and a lot more personal) than anyone else.

How to Multiply the Magic:

The "romantic card a day for a month" gesture doesn't have to be limited to just cards. You can gift your significant other with a gift a day, a flower a day, a verbalized compliment per day... the options are only limited by your imagination!

34. Invest in Scents

Many people put a lot of thought into how they want their home/apartment/living space to appear in terms of the furniture and decorations that they put into it, but a far smaller crowd considers designing the scents of their home.

Not only are you able to choose the overall scented theme of you and your significant other's home, you can also give different smells to different rooms.

You can have more invigorating scents in the places where you wake up or get energized (scents like lime, orange, and other citrus work wonders for waking up your mind). You can have more relaxing scents in your bedroom and common areas (lavender, chamomile, vanilla, or cinnamon, for example). And you can even use scents that work up an appetite.

As a rule of thumb, your bedroom, living room, and bathroom should all have their own unique scents. Anything past those choices is up to you.

You can also have certain scents be seasonal in your home. Maybe you like coconut, lime, or margarita-scented candles in the summer in your living room, but in the fall and winter months you prefer cinnamon, pumpkin, or clove-scented candles/oils/fragrances.

Whatever direction you go in with your scented interior design, feel free to either surprise your partner with the results or consult them in your decision if you think that they would appreciate being part of the process.

Watch Out For:

Not sure where to start? Fragrance stores (either perfume or candle shops) will have some surprisingly knowledgeable staff that will help you out in your journey.

35. The Engraved Gift

Give your lover an engraved personal item with a quote or a few words that mean something to the both of you.

For example, if they play guitar, get them an engraved capo. If you've been dating for a while, give them an engraved bracelet or other piece of jewelry. If they love drinking beer, give them an engraved beer mug. As always, it's important to calibrate the item to your partner.

You could have an inside joke/short phrase engraved, or the simple format of your first names with the date of when you officially became a couple.

Watch Out For:

Typos! Check, double-check, and triple-check the spelling and the words that you hand off to the engraver. And make sure you pay a trustworthy service. You don't want to find the least expensive option in town and have them mess up your beautiful gift.

36. Make a Home Video

Get your mind out of the gutter! Or, you can leave it there if you'd like. That would also be a great co-creative experience.

Does your partner travel often? Do they frequently go out of town for work?

Get in the habit of giving them cute home videos of yourself talking to them when they're away. Sure, you'll probably seem a little bit awkward when you first start recording, but that's the endearing part of it. Being able to see and hear you whenever they want (especially if there's an unfortunate time-zone difference that makes phone calls or video calls difficult to do) will make their trip that much more enjoyable.

Watch Out For:

Watch out for the dreaded shaky-handed camera. If you're taking the time to gift them a video of you, you might as well do it right. You can pick up a basic tripod for under $20 to ensure that they won't get sick watching your video. Also, if your partner travels often, you might want to learn how to use some basic editing software (just to increase the production value and flow of the videos).

How to Multiply the Magic:

Create multiple videos for them for their different moods or different times when they would want to be watching videos of you. For example, you can create one video called, "Watch this one shortly after you wake up," another called, "Watch this one when you miss me," and another called, "Watch this before your big presentation." Think of all of the times that they might want to hear your voice/see your face/have a little pep talk, and then create a dedicated video to match that moment. They will absolutely love it.

37. Give Them a Custom Fragrance

Have you ever heard of this service? It's a unique one and more common than you might think.

Grab your partner's sweaty gym shirt from the laundry basket and take it to a custom fragrance designer. The fragrance designers generally need two things: 1) a sample of what your partner naturally smells like (hence the sweaty shirt), and 2) the kind of scents that your partner generally prefers.

Watch Out For:

Make sure you can borrow the shirt without getting caught, and make sure that you know ahead of time what types of smells your partner generally gravitates towards.

38. The Custom Comic Book

Do you have a cute story as to how the two of you met? Do you vividly remember your first date? Do you have a story that you often laugh about and love to re-enact through words?

Hire a local artist or cartoonist and have a six-panel comic book drawn up of you and your partner's story. If you get someone out of animation/design school, you can likely get this done well for $100-300. All you'll have to provide is the basic story outline, any dialogue you'd like to have included, and possibly some photos of the locations that you reference in your story so that the artist can re-create them accurately in the comic.

Watch Out For:

Hiring someone whose rates seem *too* reasonable. Good artists are worth their weight in gold. It might seem ludicrous to pay someone $300-500 for a single piece of paper, but when you think of what the gesture encapsulates and how much it will mean to your significant other, you'll realize that it's worth every penny.

39. Couples Portrait Session

Organize a professional photographer to take couples photos of you—regardless of whether you have an anniversary or anything in particular to celebrate. When you look back over the course of your relationship, there's no such thing as having too many professionally captured photographs.

Loving photos of the two of you will be a nice souvenir to have of the time that you took them—they will encapsulate that stage of your relationship in beautiful, high-resolution glory.

Watch Out For:

Don't surprise your partner with this gesture last minute! They may need ample time (at least a few days, possibly a week or two) to pick out some outfits that they like or to schedule hair or nail appointments. You both want to be looking your best since you will cherish these photos for a long time to come.

How to Multiply the Magic:

If you really want to kick it up a notch, you can use this gesture as a double whammy. Organize the shoot, and once the photographer is snapping away photos and you're both as comfortable as can be, get down on one knee and propose. That's right. I said it.

If you're going to propose to your significant other, why not do it while you already have someone pointing an amazing camera at you? You can't get a much more beautiful souvenir of your special moment than high-quality photos.

40. A Storybook Ending

Write up a short story about how the two of you met (like in a children's book format) and have it professionally edited, illustrated, designed, and printed. Give it to your partner for a special occasion.

Watch Out For:

If you hire a professional illustrator (the person who draws the pictures), don't go with the cheapest option in town. Quality illustrations take time and money. So plan this gesture well in advance if you're trying to time the delivery of it with a special occasion.

41. Honor Your Muse with a Song

If you're musically inclined, write them a personalized song that mentions experiences you've had or lessons you've learned together and have it recorded professionally in a studio (it might cost anywhere from $300-$1,000, but you'll have a beautiful souvenir for life).

42. The Gift That Keeps on Giving

Does your significant other have something that they're fairly obsessed with? Designer clothes? Candles? Specialty steaks? Grooming products? Health food products? Socks?

Buy your lover a membership to a subscription service of whatever their "thing" is, and they'll receive a monthly (or quarterly) package of their favorite things in the world! Subscription services are becoming increasingly popular, and the products that are curated are often high quality and team reviewed (aka they very rarely send out any duds since they've been tested out by the same kind of aficionados as your loved one).

Watch Out For:

Be absolutely certain of two things: 1) that your significant other does, in fact, adore the thing that you're signing them up for, and 2) that the subscription service has a relatively easy return policy. As long as the subscription service isn't food related (like steak or fresh produce), the vast majority of these services have a no-hassle return policy that allows you to say "no thank you" to any of their packages. So make sure you check the fine print before you sign up!

Also, make sure you have room on whatever credit card you're using to sign up for the service. You don't necessarily have to sign up for the service forever on your partner's behalf... you can gift them with the service with a card that says, "I bought you a year of your favorite thing!" or whatever denomination of time best suits you and your partner's needs.

43. The Romance Highlight Reel

Slowly collect video footage of yourselves (either on a specific trip, on multiple trips, or over the course of your entire relationship) and have the footage edited into a cute short video put to music.

Watch Out For:

When it comes to the length of your romantic video, generally, shorter is better. A tightly cut 3-5 minute video will be better received than a 25-minute video that has painfully slow pacing. It should be edited tightly enough that you could show it to your friends/family and they would also be entertained by it (and believe me, your partner will definitely want to show it off to others). You want the video to feel like the equivalent of looking at a visual resume... as in, "Wow, look at all of the amazing things we've done together and how much we love each other!" When it comes to this gesture, quality definitely wins out over quantity. You want high-impact footage that makes your partner ask to watch it again immediately after the first time they see it.

Not much of a video editor? Totally fine! Most people aren't. Hire a university/film school student to edit it for you. You should be able to outsource the editing process to a capable video editor for anywhere from $50-200. But don't skimp too much if you decide to have someone else edit it. Remember, you and your love will likely be watching this video over a hundred times through the course of your relationship. You wouldn't hire the cheapest wedding photographer to capture your special day (because you know the images would be with you for life), and you shouldn't hire a cheap editor for your romantic video highlight reel.

How to Multiply the Magic:

Choose songs for the video that are relevant to you and your partner. Maybe you put the entire video to "your song." Maybe you only use songs by artists that you know your significant other adores. Maybe you use the song that you first slow danced to. Whatever the origins of the music, make sure it's relevant and congruent with your relationship.

You can also invest in a higher-end video editor (likely in the $500-1,500 range) who will create custom titles (the pages with words throughout your video) and make sure that the video edits are timed to the music. As long as you pick someone whose demo reel you can scope out beforehand, video editing is definitely an industry where you get what you pay for.

Final note. Personally, I think that the best romantic highlight reels are created when you take footage that spans a significant length of time. So pick up a camera that you can easily shoot video with and start storing away footage of the two of you and your adventures sooner rather than later. That way, when you come to edit/give the footage to the editor, you have years of memories that you can condense into a beautiful, romantic reminder of all of the fun that you two have shared together. The video, when revealed to your partner, creates a uniquely unparalleled feeling of, "This is our story, and we're creating it one day at a time."

Quality Time and Connection

Does your partner really light up when it's just the two of you, slowing down, removing all distractions, and just *being* with each other? Then this section is for you!

44. Fireplace, Wine, and Cuddling

This is a favorite date for my girlfriend and me. And it's just as simple as it sounds.

Remove your physical layers of ego by stripping down to your underwear (or less), grabbing a bottle of wine (or other favorite beverage), and sitting in front of a fireplace (if you have access to one). If there's no fireplace to be found, making a big comfy pit out of pillows, blankets, and other soft things will do. Then surround your homemade pillow pit with lots of candlelight. What you're really after is creating a soft, comfortable space where you can be soft and comfortable with each other.

Lots of eye gazing, deep conversations, extended kisses, touching, and tenderness is in order.

Watch Out For:

The fire hazard! Don't let anything get near the open flames or your hot date might end with a call to the firefighters.

How to Multiply the Magic:

Have some of your partner's favorite snacks on hand to feed each other (finger foods that don't require plates or cutlery are generally best for this situation).

45. Spoiling Sessions

Want to reconnect with your partner on a physical and sexual level?

Spoiling sessions are one of my absolute favorite things to prescribe to my clients who are in relationships.

A spoiling session is a 30-45 minute block of time where you or your partner is afforded the opportunity to ask for whatever you want. Whether that looks like a 45-minute full body coconut oil massage, various forms of cuddling, a specific sexual position, uninterrupted oral sex, or all of the above, it's your time to ask for and receive what you want from your loving partner.

Not only do spoiling sessions allow the receiving partner to tap into exactly what they want moment to moment, it also builds their verbal courage as they get used to asking for what they want. There will be a certain amount of anxiety that comes along with doing this for the first time (as many people are conditioned to believe that being sexually "selfish" is a negative thing), but it will help you grow as an individual and as a couple.

Nervous about the silence? You can always create a 30-45 minute playlist of your favorite music to relax you even further into the exercise.

How to Multiply the Magic:

Have your favorite massage oils, sex toys, blindfolds, and anything else on hand that your sexy little mind can think up.

46. Ask These 10 Questions to Go Deeper in Your Intimacy

Emotionally reconnect as a couple by setting aside time to ask each other these ten deep questions in one sitting:

1. Is there anything I can do for you in this moment to help you feel more comfortable or loved?
2. How can I better support you in your life?
3. Is there anything I have done in the past week that may have unknowingly hurt you?
4. When you come home from work, what can I do or say that will make you feel the most loved?
5. Is there any kind of physical touch that I can engage in more that helps you to feel loved?
6. Do you think you will need more closeness or more alone time over the next couple of days?
7. Is there any argument that we had this past week that you feel incomplete about?
8. How do you feel about our sex life lately?
9. What are the main stressors currently in your life, and is there any way can I alleviate that stress for you, if only a small amount?

10. When do you find speaking difficult and how can I best support you through those moments?

Watch Out For:

For best results, clear out all of the distractions from your environment. Turn off your phones, close the laptops, and switch off the TV. Make sure the kids are asleep and the dog is taken care of. Clear out anything that could potentially ping its way into the space that you are creating and handle it ahead of time.

47. Art Night In

Everyone has a creative side! In most cultures, artistic expression is missing from daily living. This is a great way to infuse some creative juices back into your love life. Creativity also reawakens parts of your mind that can feel somewhat dormant when they are underused… so this gesture has the added benefit of making you both a little bit smarter (just when you thought it wasn't possible).

This can be a creative date where you buy a canvas or two, some basic colored paints, and paint together in your house (with newspaper on the ground). A couple bottles of red or white wine will help to get the creativity flowing.

Watch Out For:

Getting paint everywhere! Put newspaper down on the ground and use a water-soluble paint. Also, make sure that you both wear clothes that you don't mind getting paint on.

48. Make a Co-Creative Vision Board

Pick up an assortment of new magazines and create a joint vision board for what your future will look like together. This activity is great for connecting you by creating a tangible joint vision for the future. You get to co-create and witness your future together via magazine clippings... it's like staring into the future!

Watch Out For:

Have a wide enough variety of magazines that you'll both have things you're excited to cut out and include on the board. Make sure you have magazines that cover your favorite things and theirs.

49. Learn a New Style Of Dance... Then Surprise Them With It!

Secretly take dancing lessons in a new style of dance that neither of you knows (any style of ballroom dancing like the waltz, tango, salsa, West Coast swing, rumba, or cha cha will work perfectly) and then teach your significant other how to do the style of dance once you feel proficient at it.

Watch Out For:

If you really have two left feet, make sure you drop in for at least five to ten classes so that you can get a good, foundational grasp on it.

50. Turn Your Home into a Bed & Breakfast

Turn your house into a bed and breakfast for a full weekend (where you two are the only guests).

Go for long walks in your neighborhood (or somewhere beautiful in nature if it's available to you), make breakfast every morning for them and serve it to them in bed, and spend your days cuddling, talking about your dreams in life, and reconnecting as a couple.

Watch Out For:

Make sure that you handle all distractions in your regular lives that would keep you both from being able to fully drop in and enjoy the experience. Make sure that neither of you has to work, and remove all obligations outside of the home. Really commit to enjoying the best "staycation" you could ever imagine.

How to Multiply the Magic:

Hire a private chef to make your meals for you (or just to make your breakfasts) so that you get to enjoy extra time with your lover, and you don't have to worry about the logistics of meal preparation.

A Reminder to Take Action

Those are the fifty powerful romantic gestures in all of their glory.

But remember... they remain words on a page until you decide to take action.

So the thing to do now is pick your two or three favorite gestures, put them in your private calendar, and start to take action steps to make them a reality.

The best wisdom in the world will simply remain words unless it is met with action. So please, for the love of love, for the love of your relationship, for the love of your ever-emerging best self... take action on your favorite romantic gesture within the next week or two. My guess is that you'll have such a massively positive response from your significant other that you'll want to keep doing more of the gestures for them. But it all starts with that one.

So take the first step. You (and your partner) will be glad you did.

Want to Become the Ultimate Relationship Partner?

Want to ensure that you always have the kind of relationship that can endure anything?

Get a free gift when you hop on to my personal mailing list and get weekly updates with new relationship building tips.

Go to www.JordanGrayConsulting.com for your free gift now!

One Last Thing

If this book has helped you in any way, please do me a quick favor and give it a short review on Amazon. It not only helps me in my writing of future books, but also helps me reach others with my work. I really appreciate you taking just a few moments of your time to share your feedback.

Other Books by Jordan Gray

Keep Her Captivated: Lead Your Relationship to Its Maximum Potential	http://amzn.to/1dyUPBH
50 Powerful Date Ideas: Brag-Worthy, Cost-Effective Dates from a Professional Dating Coach	http://amzn.to/1Iu19r8
The Introvert's Guide to Dating	http://amzn.to/1KtFGAc
Overcoming Intimacy Anxiety: How to Love When Loving Someone Scares You	http://amzn.to/1T7xzuz

About the Author

Jordan Gray is a best-selling author and relationship coach who helps people remove their emotional blocks and maintain thriving intimate relationships.

His thoughts on modern dating and relationships have been featured in numerous print publications and on radio and television broadcasts internationally.

In his relationship coaching practice, Jordan has worked with thousands of students over the past six years, and has more wedding invitations from his former clients than he can keep up with.

When he's not coaching clients or writing new books, Jordan loves to surf without a wetsuit, immerse himself in new cultures, and savor slow-motion hangouts with his closest companions.

You can see more of his writing at:
www.JordanGrayConsulting.com

Printed in Great Britain
by Amazon